precisely how to
TAKE CARE OF YOUR SELF

precisely how to

TAKE CARE OF YOUR SELF

by Earl Jabay

LOGOS INTERNATIONAL
Plainfield, New Jersey

Precisely How to Take Care of Your Self
Copyright © 1979 by Logos International
All rights reserved
Printed in the United States of America
Library of Congress Catalog Card Number: 78-71526
International Standard Book Number: 0-88270-346-3
Logos International, Plainfield, New Jersey 07060

Earl Jabay is a pastor in the Reformed Church in America and a chaplain at the New Jersey Neuro-Psychiatric Institute, Princeton, New Jersey.

1715

by Earl Jabay

Search for Identity
The God-Players
The Kingdom of Self

Contents

precisely how to
TAKE CARE OF YOUR SELF

1

A Book About the Care of Your Self

"Take care of yourself!"

This is what a friend often says to you in parting. The words are seldom taken literally, but they are warm words and we like to hear them.

The small volume in your hand is an attempt to take these words seriously and respond to that command: "Take care of yourself!" I deeply believe that if a few of us would really take care of ourselves as God wants, the whole world would begin to change.

But *how* does one take care of oneself?

To this question, people give three basically different answers.

Most people are do-it-yourselfers. This kind of person claims to be self-sufficient in the face of his problems. If such people need any help in their lives, *they* will do it. Independency to them is a virtue made necessary by the fact that one really cannot trust another human being. One must care for *himself* because who else can do it as well?

Such people are blind and do not know it. Their lives are increasingly filled with self-centeredness. They also resent others who fail to recognize their superior self-knowledge.

The second answer as to how a human being takes care of himself is given by those who have placed themselves under "professional care." The professional is looked upon as a person blessed with unusual maturity and a keen knowledge of what makes people tick. The weary client, after cloaking the therapist with a messianic mantle, proceeds to undress his mind before the searching eye of his counselor. The professional person gradually makes it clear to his client that he alone can rid himself of his shameful immaturities and learn to stand on his own two feet.

Both of these methods—independency and dependency—fail to truly care for the self.

But what else *is* there?

There is God!—and we ought to do nothing before making a central place for Him in our lives. After that, we need to learn from Him how to properly care for ourselves.

We know, also, that God will have nothing to do with the extremes of independency and dependency. What He wants is *inter-dependency* among people who believe in Him. And now I am talking about something called *shepherding*.

Shepherding is the word we will use for the mutual, spiritual care two Christians give each other. Shepherding is a Christian inviting another Christian to speak a word from the Lord.

Now before you get the wrong idea, this is *not* a book for

pastors on how to take care of their people. I am not trying to add anything to the courses which seminaries offer on how to "tend the flock of God." Nor am I addressing the leaders in the charismatic movement who use the term *shepherding* to describe the guidance and oversight they give to their followers. I really have very little to say about the pastor-parishioner or teacher-student models of shepherding.

My effort in this book is to lay out a proven method whereby two lay Christians of the same sex are taught the principles of mutual spiritual care. This shared caring of persons is called shepherding.

Shepherding is God's method of getting things done in our lives. He promised: "If two of you agree on earth about anything they ask, it will be done" (Matt. 18:19 RSV). Our Lord promises to be present when two or three believers are gathered in His Name. There is no better way to take care of ourselves than in that kind of healing fellowship.

Come along with me now as an observer of a meeting between the Lord, a shepherd and a sheep.

2

A Shepherd and His Sheep

S—Shepherd
s—sheep

S: Greetings. Nice to see you. Please sit down. Let's get right to work.

s: Thanks.

S: Our last meeting was a month ago. Anything to report on since then? Tell me the good news first.

s: I quit smoking! Haven't had any cigarettes for two weeks now. I never thought I could go that long without the weed. It's a nice surprise, even to myself. And I like this new freedom. But I have to watch myself—especially after meals.

S: This is good news. I could not be happier if it had happened to myself. And it did, about fifteen years ago when I could not stand myself any more as a smoker. So—we are both free! Praise God!

s: Yes, praise God!

S: (long pause) Take a look at the rest of your life now. Is there any place where you are failing?

s: Yes, there is. But I'm not ready to talk about it.

S: Then we'll wait. We have an agreement not to push each other into things for which we are not ready. You know that.

s: Wait—changed my mind—let's talk.

(pause)

I'm eating like a pig.

I'm not smoking but I make up for it with food. You can't see it yet but I've already gained seven pounds. I just know I'll keep going up. Somehow this is worse to talk about than smoking.

S: I hear you.

But look—God gave you victory over smoking. He is the key to the food problem as well.

s: You can talk. You don't have the problem.

S: I've got other problems—just as bad.

(pause)

Are you ready to do something about the problem or do you want to be fat?

s: I'm ready.

S: Ready for what?

s: Ready to stop eating.

S: That's a little extreme.

s: No—I'm serious. I'll go on a fast. It's quicker. Gets the job done. Why fool around?

S: I disagree.

May I make a suggestion?

(s nods affirmatively)

Sit down with your wife and plan the menus for one week—that's twenty-one menus. Limit yourself to fifteen hundred calories per day. Eliminate all junk food, high-calorie desserts and between-meal snacks. When you and your wife are agreed on the menus, call me on the telephone and read it off to me to make sure you are eating right. Then, when you are ready, use the diet for one week only. After that you can eat like a pig again or make another agreement. What do you say?

s: Well, I need help. I'm ready.

S: You need time to work this out with your wife. Let me know when you have the menus worked out. When will I hear from you?

s: In a week.

S: That's too long. How about three days?

s: Okay, three days. Agreed.

S: You've had about a half hour to talk now. Let's change hats.

Here I want to interrupt this meeting of three—the Lord, the Shepherd and the sheep—to point out what is happening. Very quickly, notice the following:

• Shepherding, you can see, is very business-like. The meeting has structure, content and purpose.

• The Shepherd takes charge of the meeting. He leads. He is *supposed* to!

• The Shepherd shares in the joy of the sheep's victory over himself.

• The Shepherd questions the sheep where he is failing, where he is a sinner needing help.

• The Shepherd never pushes, never coerces. He only makes suggestions. That is the only power he has. The Holy Spirit alone moves minds and hearts.

• The Shepherd does not hesitate to disagree with the sheep, nor does the Shepherd allow the sheep to be vague and indefinite.

• The Shepherd suggests a mutually agreed upon plan of action—in this case an approved diet—rather than to think of new ideas and have new feelings. Also, the agreement is limited to a week and the sheep chooses when to begin.

• Finally, observe that the meeting closes with the Shepherd relinquishing his role and now becoming a sheep! This is the most basic and necessary qualification of a Shepherd—that he also be a sheep to the very person he had as his sheep!

Now let us continue to observe this meeting of three. Remember that the Shepherd and sheep have reversed roles.

S: Do you have anything to raise?

s: Nothing.

S: Let's just wait. Something will come.

s: Nothing.

S: (pause) Will you check your relationship with your boss, your co-workers, your wife, your children, your neighbors? Is there any anger or resentment toward these?

s: No.

(long pause)

I've got a problem with a schoolteacher that we might look at. This teacher is the woman who teaches my ten-year-old daughter Judy. She's sort of special.

S: I remember her.

s: This teacher is new in the school and still getting used to the kids. Well, she decided that Judy wasn't paying attention and right in front of the class, told her she was lazy. Judy denied it and then the teacher called her disrespectful! This really shook up my Judy, and she came home crying. The teacher sent a note home with Judy, asking for a conference.

The whole thing made me boiling mad!

S: At whom?

s: Well, the teacher, of course! None of these teachers today know what they are doing! So my wife and I went to the school for a conference. It was a bad, bad day. I got angry with the teacher for picking on Judy and embarrassing her in front of the whole class. Then, to make matters worse, my wife agreed with the teacher! There I was battling both of them and getting nowhere.

I've about given up. Let the females run the world! They are welcome to it. (a long, sullen pause)

S: Well, do you want my reaction or shall we drop the matter? I do have a suggestion to make.

s: Make it!

S: Go tell the teacher you made a mistake and will support her 100 percent.

s: Are you *crazy*?!

S: Let me tell you why I suggest an apology.

First of all, you're blind to Judy. The girl most likely *is* lazy and disrespectful. The teacher cared enough to rebuke Judy openly. What's wrong with that? You should thank this teacher for doing her job!

s: My Judy didn't need to be embarrassed that way!

S: So what is wrong with punishing a child when she is wrong? What Judy needs is some tough love, someone who loves her enough to oppose her.

s: Well, I love her.

S: I know you do. I believe you. But I also believe you love your Judy more than your wife. Any man who votes with his daughter against his wife, loves his daughter more than his wife. That's bad for the marriage and bad for the child.

s: (long pause) I've got to think about this.
S: When shall we meet again?
s: Let's make it in two weeks. I'll think this over.
S: Let's have prayer.
(Both men pray for each other's needs.)

Regarding the second half of the meeting, notice the following:
• The sheep draws a blank, but the Shepherd waits him out.
• The sheep really has unloaded a complex and difficult problem on the Shepherd. Without understanding the dynamics of the problem, the Shepherd is led by the Holy Spirit to see the need for an apology. The Shepherd senses that to really help the sheep, he must stand lovingly against him.
• The suggestion to make an apology is absolutely safe and wise. Only the sheep's egoism will be damaged.
• The meeting ends on a heavy and rather sad note. Praise God! The Holy Spirit is *the* Counselor to work in the hearts of both men. Not all problems need to be solved in one meeting.

3

How God Introduced Me to Shepherding

My work as a mental hospital chaplain began in the early 1960s. It was my task to minister to the spiritual needs of about four hundred patients. In addition, local clergymen with emotional problems increasingly reached out to me for help. I had plenty to keep me busy.

It was not the work load, however, which gave me difficulty. My problem, I soon realized, was *myself*. I, too, was a needy person. I needed someone to counsel *me*.

My psychological training told me the best place to go for help was to a good psychiatrist. It was not long before I was in treatment with one of the best trained psychiatrists in New York City. The therapy went on for two and a half years. I liked him and he liked me. I was motivated. Both of us worked hard. Result: I became more depressed. Also, I reluctantly realized that psychiatry was a dead-end street. It is a conviction I have never since had reason to doubt. See

Chapter 6 for more on that.

God then sent new people into my life through my hospital ministry. They were the men and women of Alcoholics Anonymous. How were these people helped? Not by the professionals but by each other. Every member had a sponsor with whom he worked a program called the Twelve Steps. God, moreover, was the key to success with them. I knew this was finally a road that went somewhere.

Late in 1963, I decided to ask a brother pastor to be my pastor. Dr. G. was a wise old man, a retired missionary. I told him I wanted to do what my alcoholic patients were doing. They were practicing a spiritual program which began with a fearless moral inventory of their lives. At first the old man was caught off balance, protesting that he "didn't do that kind of work." When I explained further, however, he switched completely by announcing that he had a few sins of his own to confess! Unfortunately, my new pastor moved out of state to a retirement home soon after we began meeting.

I went next to Father Ed, a Roman Catholic priest, asking him to be my pastor. Here was a man of God who understood a pastor's need for a pastor. Father Ed visited his superior regularly. At such times he would enter the confessional and receive counsel. Finally, I had a man who himself was under the care of someone. Our arrangement worked beautifully for a couple of years. Then Father Ed was transferred to a distant parish and, once again, I was a sheep with no shepherd.

By this time, the idea of shepherding was becoming clear to me. The Lord was allowing me to see a number of things:

(1) Spiritual help and guidance is a two-way street. One

should receive it from the same person to whom it is offered. The old psychiatric model of an all-wise, healthy professional helping the emotional cripple is, I feel, fundamentally unworkable. Both the person helped and the helper need to be under God's authority and each other's spiritual care.

THE PSYCHIATRIC MODEL   THE SHEPHERDING MODEL

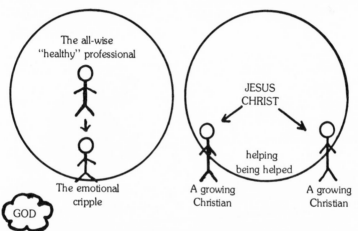

The all-wise "healthy" professional

The emotional cripple

JESUS CHRIST

helping being helped

A growing Christian   A growing Christian

GOD

(2) A regular opportunity to "confess your sins to one another" (James 5:16) is an essential part of Christian growth. My initial doubts and fears in doing this were swept away when it was suggested I begin with "little sins."

(3) Everyone needs someone to lovingly react to his life with good advice, helpful criticism and, in some cases, rebuke. One should begin with small revelations of himself. As love and trust grow, so will the freedom to disclose oneself.

(4) Obedience to the Lord is not only a state of mind. Obedience is a concrete action which usually runs counter to

one's own desire. The suggestion unto action, it is true, may come directly from the Lord but we need also to make room for the suggestion to come from the Lord through another person.

After Father Ed's departure, I went to a brother pastor and explained the idea of shepherding. "Let's try it and see how it goes," he said. So we proceeded on a test basis.

The days of testing are long since finished. We have reached some conclusions, many of which are set forth in this book.

We are both in agreement that shepherding is an effective, helpful way to grow in the Christian life.

We know that God is the answer. And we know we need limits, guidance, containment and security.

This is what shepherding is all about.

4

Our Basic Problem in Life

There is really only one basic problem with us.

In its simplest form, the problem is that we displace God. We move from under His authority and power to a position of being under none but our own. The effect of this folly is that we live in the delusion that the human ego is the highest power and authority in the world. Someone put it this way: "I finally realized my problem was that I was occupying a throne in my life which was intended only for Jesus Christ."

In this state of mind, one may not always feel as powerful as God Almighty, but he must certainly pretend to do the work of the Almighty. After all, who else will accomplish the great tasks in life if not the person himself? It follows, too, that the Almighty's job is then to *help*—but not control—the egoist as he tries his best to live out this fantasy at the center of his life.

To make matters worse, we all lie about this great lie in our lives. With an innocent and straight face we all proclaim: "Me? Play god? Never! I'm a weak and struggling person and besides, I believe in Almighty God."

Here we are looking straight into the face of the great lie. This, truly, is the father of them all.

Even psychotic people, you know, are more honest than that. Dozens of psychotic people have flatly told me, as mental hospital chaplain, that they are God or Jesus Christ. They had no doubts or questions about it. Each one had thought deeply about the issue and there was no other conclusion: "I am God and, therefore, I play God." This was their "truth" and they believed it to the depth of their souls.

And these psychotic people are right! They *are* gods, the way they have set up their worlds. If the true and living God is "exiled" from their lives, this leaves the next highest power—themselves—to play god. And, of course, that's wrong, but at least it's honest to admit it.

The same cannot be said for us "normal" people. We have added dishonesty to our wrongness. In actual life we live on the delusion that we are gods, but then we cover this lie with another lie, the lie that we are not deluded.

Could it be that, through these so-called psychotic people, God intends to teach us not to lie?

Let me give you a simple example of how the great, delusional lie works.

A man came to me for counsel who was struggling with alcoholism. He was losing the struggle and was going downhill, but the morning we talked, he was sober. After laying out the problem again in detail, he leaned back and reflected on his life. He said: "I guess I'm still too weak—or maybe I'm not weak enough."

The first half of this statement was a restatement of a life-long delusion, sustained by bottomless self-pity and resentment. The second half—"maybe I'm not weak enough"—was the truth. The truth was that he had built his life on the lying pretense that he was *strong*—strong enough to control himself and alcohol, which he could never do. He assumed that he was his own highest power. This was a lie.

But how can we be sure that the lie is the core problem with this alcoholic person?

Simply by the results. When he lied to himself that he was too weak, he drank. Once he faced the truth about his unbelievably strong willfulness and self-centeredness, he went on to repent of his sin and surrender his will to God. Recovering alchololics put it this way: "You stop lying, you'll stop drinking." It is true.

Until one deals with the spiritual issues of alcoholism, he will not understand it because alcoholism is basically a god problem. If one can discern and accept that fact, then something else will become clear: that there is really only *one* problem in life. From this one problem, all other problems flow: emotional disorders, addictions, suicidal tendencies, marital discord, antisocial behavior, many physical problems, depression, rebellion, etc. These are all symptoms of the problem which is the great lie that I am a god.

Notice that the symptoms of the problem all have one thing in common: a state of being out of control. No matter how much will power or want power a person musters, he finds he is losing the battle. So, therefore, we say to anyone who wants to live again:

> Those who try to be in control,
> fly out of control
> until they come under Control.

This short sentence summarizes the three great stages of life which God wants us to pass through:

> Stage One: "I'll run my own life."
> Stage Two: "I can't stop myself."
> Stage Three: "I give up—I surrender to God."

Life is a journey which begins in self-centeredness, proceeds to chaotic self-destruction and, by the grace and mercy of God, can end in Christ-centeredness.

So it is either self or God who is the highest power and authority. Both cannot be ultimate. Having two gods just does not work. God built us for monotheism. Catherine of Siena was right: "Nothing is more His enemy than is self to me—It will be God or self, not God and self."

What has the problem to do with shepherding?

At least two things.

One of the greatest problems in being a committed, egocentric god-player is that it is such a lonely position in the world. God is "exiled" and there is a natural estrangement between the god-player and the troublesome human race. He must constantly fight them off to remain elevated. The sense of loneliness is indescribable as we all know from our own experience.

Shepherding deals directly with the problem of loneliness. The self is helped to be under the authority and rule of Jesus Christ while at the same time being *with* a fellow believer. The two happen simultaneously. Loneliness is impossible with Christ as Lord and a fellow believer at one's side.

Secondly, shepherding is the most direct way of

countering our egocentricity which is the problem. In shepherding, the sheep asks the Lord to speak to him through the shepherd. Sometimes the shepherd will support and encourage him, but at other times he must oppose and even correct him. There are certain times too, when the problem in us is so great that nothing else will do than a command to stop in the name of the Lord.

Can one Christian really say that to another?

Who else will?

Quite frankly, our traditional authorities have piteously weak voices today. We are all aware of the breakdown of authority in the home and church—the two bodies to which we especially look for guidance and the rules for life. The rules for living today are written in pencil, hardly legible and easily erased. The limits of our behavior are marked by a cord made out of rubber.

What else can a Christian do today than turn to a fellow believer and vest him with authority from God? "Where two or three are gathered together in my name, there am I in the midst of them" (Matt. 18:20). In such a meeting, there takes place a binding of behavior, a loosing of sins and a promise that if two Christians make agreements on earth, they are honored in heaven.

5

God's Solution to the Problem of Life

God's solution to man's problem is to give us the *truth*. Only the truth will destroy our delusions.

The truth is that the kingdom of self must go. This massive delusion we have fabricated must die. We are not kings and queens, nor were we ever intended to be kings and queens. It was sheer insanity for us even to presume that we could rule ourselves. Can a dog be his own master? Can a field plough itself? Can stone shape itself into a statue? Can a sick person be his own surgeon? Can a person be his own god?

True, the delusion of self-rule had filled our minds with exciting fantasies. We often had glimpses of ourselves as right when everyone else was wrong, as superior when everyone else was very ordinary, as brave when everyone else was timid. Sometimes we amazed ourselves with our clear perception of a problem and our brilliant solution to it. Even during some unhappy days when everything seemed to be going wrong, we were not defeated. We always felt that a little more hard work and determination would see us through. A vision of triumphant success was always before us. But it was all fantasy.

The truth was that we bore a false witness to ourselves. We were constantly in conflict with people, especially our authorities. In certain areas, we were completely out of control—a few of us were alcoholics but others were food-oholics or work-oholics and all of us knew that we could put "--oholic" on the end of a dozen words, applying each of them to us. We were big on talk, small on follow-through and action. Life was heavy and the burden of it frightened us. There was no meaning to life. Nor was God around. We knew we were alone—and defeated.

This is the picture of every man. It is the reason why the kingdom of self must go.

But how?

By voluntary dethronement. By casting our crowns before the feet of the King of kings and Lord of lords.

And it slays us.

Dethronement registers with us as death. Self-rule and all the delusions that go with it, are dearer than life itself. I saw this in a young medical student who got into medical school but soon began to drop behind his class. Finally, he washed out. He had tried his best but it was not enough. The dream of becoming a medical doctor, however, was impossible to give up. It was either medical school or death—and since he could not go back to school, he chose death. Fortunately, the attempt at suicide failed. He is alive today and has made a good adjustment to himself as a man of limited ability, rather than the man of his dreams. In the great crisis of his life, however, the dream was dearer than life.

Self dethronement is the last thing we are ready to give God. Anything but that. What God wants, we are least willing to give. God wants our wills and our most cherished ideas about ourselves and He wants them dead. How will this ever happen?

Well, it would never happen except for the sovereign grace of God. With a divine mercy which always leaves us puzzled about its working, the Holy Spirit breaks through the gates of our miserable kingdoms and touches our spirits. The Spirit of God graciously regenerates us. It is all beyond explanation. But this we know: were it not for the grace and love of God, all kings in the kingdom of self would perish in self-destruction. The course of such kingdoms is predictable. It is sure death, for the wages of sin is death.

When once the regenerating Spirit of God touches the human spirit, there is a response of self-surrender. The wandering, discontented spirit of a person is finally set "in place" and at rest under the strong, loving authority of God. One person put it this way: "I've been in a rush all my life but didn't know where I was going. It was a race to nowhere. God pulled me over—and I was never so glad to be stopped. I'm still stopped. My racing, rushing days are finished." Someone else had a similar experience: "I always believed that when you got to the end of your rope, you tied a knot in it and hung on. Then a friend said: 'Let go, let God.' I finally did, and fell all of half an inch to a solid rock. I knew it was God I had touched. I cried. I was home at last."

Both of these new persons in Christ had to die to their self-centeredness. Note carefully that the self does not die. It is careless to speak of "the death of the self." The experience of self-surrender registers with the self as a death experience but this is only because the delusional world is so dear to us that we fear we cannot live without it. I have a friend who is a heavy cigarette smoker. He wants to quit. Why does he continue to smoke? He is blocked by his delusion, a delusion which tells him he will possibly die if he quits. Do not smokers say they are "dying for a cigarette"? I know, of course, he will not die. He will live in a new way. So I told my friend: "Die. Get it over with."

What we are looking at here is "the way of the cross." The cross always means death. But *what* in a person dies when he becomes a Christian? It is self-will. It is our bitterest death, this coming under the will of Jesus Christ. Obedience to Christ means the Christian's will is broken. He no longer gets his way. He defers to Christ's will.

Therefore, self-will dies in the "way of the cross." Was it not so with our Lord? He drank the cup of suffering and endured a slow death on the cross only because it was the Father's will.

We are to follow in His footsteps.

The way of the cross is not the way of death. It is the road to life, to Christ who is the life. In Him we possess it all.

But in ourselves, we possess nothing at all of His life until we surrender. I was in the Christian ministry ten years before I surrendered to Christ. How could I have gone through a seminary and stood in a pulpit for ten years and not be surrendered? I have no rational explanation. All I can say is that I was lost in my delusion.

But now I want to say what all this has to do with shepherding. Two things.

The first is that in the shepherd-sheep relationship, the

shepherd must begin his work by asking for the unconditional surrender (or re-surrender) of the sheep to Jesus Christ. Do not take this for granted in anyone. Look at it this way. When you sell a house, the last thing you do is turn over the keys to the new owner. Many Christians have told Christ that they want Him as the new owner of their spiritual house, but they have never turned over the keys to Him. It is the task of a shepherd to ask for the keys and, in the name of Jesus Christ, receive them. Here is an illustration of what I mean:

S: This is our first visit. I want to check with you where you are with Jesus Christ. Have you ever consciously resigned as the highest power of your life and asked Jesus Christ to be your highest power?

s: Well, I was confirmed in my church when I was fourteen. I guess that was a sign of where I stood.

S: I'm not asking where you stood. I'm asking if you ever surrendered, if you ever turned yourself in to Christ.

s: I hope I have.

S: That's not enough. We have to make sure. Can we agree today that you unconditionally surrender to Jesus Christ?

s: I want to.

S: God accepts you. It is agreed.

The second comment I want to make about self-surrender is this: after the initial surrender, it needs to be repeated time and time and time again. There is so much unsurrendered territory in even the most consecrated Christian, that even with a lifetime of spiritual discipline, only a small beginning will be made. The most serious delusion among Christians today is that the kingdom of self is destroyed once we have accepted Jesus Christ. The truth is that with the coming of the kingdom of God, Jesus Christ establishes a bridgehead in the vast wasteland of our kingdom of self, but the enemy territory in us is never completely conquered in this life. Christ's occupation of the areas controlled by self is usually far less complete than we are ready to admit.

Shepherding is a method by which we regularly and continuously surrender more of the kingdom of self to the kingdom of God.

6

Man's Solution to the Problem of Life

At this point, I must say something about modern psychology. It has become the religion of the masses and, even though one theory contradicts another, it is looked to for the solutions to most all our problems. This is a new age of faith—faith in the behavioral sciences.

Psychological science is dedicated to what it deeply believes: man is the highest power in the world. Man is ultimate and, therefore, God is dead. Such a conclusion is unavoidable because it is nonsense to speak of two ultimates. Facing that fact, Christians are beginning to see that psychology (dedicated to the self) and Christianity (dedicated to God) are in basic conflict.

I want to explain why psychology and God do not mix.

Psychology says: "Try this new therapy. It is the newest thing out. It will make you a stronger person." But God says: "If you touch it, be prepared to do it all yourself. I don't need your 'help.' I need your helplessness, your surrender. Your surrender is proof to me of your understanding that I am God and you are a human being."

Psychology says: "Find yourself. We will help you do this." God says: "Come to the end of yourself. Give up on yourself, decisively. You cannot remake the old you. I have better plans for you."

Psychology says: "We will help you feel better about yourself. After all, what's more important?" But God says: "Just do my will, which is usually different from your will. You'll be better after you do it."

Psychology says: "You are solvent as a person!" God says: "You are bankrupt as a person."

Psychology says: "It's up to you. Only you can do it." But God says: "Only divine power can straighten out your twisted life. It is *not* up to you. Everything hangs on Me, not you."

It can't be both ways. One cannot fight and surrender at the same time.

Many of my colleagues in the ministry do not agree with my position. They feel that one should psychologize Christianity. Their idea is to take whatever psychological knowledge that has appeal and absorb it into Christian counseling. Though clergymen speak of a dialogue with the behaviorial scientists, the speaking is all done by the scientists to the pastors because that's the way the pastors want it. The pastoral counselors I know are like sponges, busily absorbing the juices they are squeezing out of the human potential movement, sensitivity training, reality therapy, encounter groups, behavior modification, transactional analysis, assertiveness training and so forth. These "precious" juices are highly valued. When they are mixed with the waters of

Christian truth, we are told, they bring healing and health!

Mark me down as one pastor who no longer believes that.

I see this "drink" as new participation in the idolatry of self. Once again, the self helps himself become strong. This only postpones surrender to God. Granted, such an approach gives us token help—just enough to keep us coming back for more. But this help also effectively cuts us off from the power of the Savior.

Our obedience to the Savior is best offered through a non-professional, Christian believer who is himself under obedience to God through the very person he is advising.

We call this method *shepherding*. It is an attempt in the problems of life to rise above the countless false solutions which continually urge us to try a little harder.

I believe God will soon send the professional counselors—along with their servile pastors—on their way. Their day is coming to an end. It's too late for what they do. The arrangement never did work. Christian counselors, on the other hand, are beginning to see the light, as one man said: "I've wasted a good deal of time in the psychological deserts. It was hard to admit that my work was more secular than sacred."

It is time for lay shepherds to guide their sheep into the path of obedience, both shepherds and sheep being led by the Holy Spirit.

So let us abandon our hope in all the recent discoveries in the field of humanistic knowledge. Without God, none of it works. With God, who needs it?

Our hope is in God.

7

Finding the
Purpose of Life

Think with me for a moment about the great purpose of your life and mine. Why are we here on this planet?

A businessman said to me: "Life is basically competition. Survival of the fittest. I plan to survive." Is that what it is all about? Hardly.

I knew a man once who believed life was basically a party. His purpose was to enjoy himself—and that's all. Seems to me that would become terribly hard work after a while.

Did God place us here to expand our knowledge? Is that the purpose of life? Indeed not. Our knowledge will always be embarrassingly small and shot through with error.

Were you sent into the world to leave a lasting mark? Except for a very few people, our names are completely forgotten in four generations, even by our descendants.

Is serving mankind the purpose of life? True, certain individuals may inspire us to such service, but mankind in

31

general is to most of us a sad disappointment. It is seldom that any of us, having read the daily newspaper, rise to serve mankind.

Could it be that we are here to "glorify God and enjoy Him forever," as the Westminster Confession states? There is something which must precede that, as we'll see.

Someone once told me that his purpose in life was "to find out who I am." I told him his wife, a terribly neglected woman, had already answered that question correctly dozens of times, if he would only listen to her. He did not appreciate my humor.

Sometimes religious people say their purpose in life is to praise and thank God. But God is saddened by our praise if we have not first given Him what *He* wants. And He does not want praise first of all.

Is it, perhaps, the purpose of our lives to recognize and acknowledge God? No. Even the devils do that.

Others have suggested that our purpose in life is to solve our problems, achieve happiness, find truth, achieve righteousness and the list could go on.

None of these answers have the ring of truth in them.

If my understanding is correct, God intends something both simple and profound with each of us.

His purpose with us is this: *to find God as the highest power in our lives*.

You may say: "But I always *knew* that!"

No. We did not always know that. No one "knows it" until we go out of control enough times to make us surrender the controls of our lives to God. Until our surrender to God is decisive and continuous, we remain the highest power in our lives.

So thank God that you are among those who have lost control of their lives to God—through overeating, overwork, alcohol, divorce, depression, compulsions, temper tantrums, migraine headaches, ulcers, etc. A person who had a severe emotional breakdown said to me: "I'm glad I went off my rocker. I was completely out of my mind. It was hell, and I could not do a thing about it. So I asked God to please do *something*, anything. And He did. Today I am alive, but it's different. I'm not the same. God never left me. He is still the power in my life."

Shepherding is a concrete device to make place for God to remain in our lives as our highest power.

By allowing another person to represent God to us, we make place for His power and authority.

And that's the purpose of our brief visit on this planet.

8

The Easiest Road to Freedom

Once God is found and obeyed, the self must turn away from the care of the self, for this is the task of the Lord himself.

What I mean is that the self must no longer discipline the self. Our long effort to be self-disciplined must end. A weary man once said to me: "What's wrong with me? I don't even have the self-discipline to stop biting my fingernails!" Hundreds of people have asked me: "How can I develop the self-discipline to get along with people?"

I say to such people: "Forget self-discipline. It's the wrong road. Besides, it is impossibly difficult. But there is a better and easier way."

"What *is* it?"

"The easiest way," I suggest, "is to come directly under the authority of God and His Word by coming under the discipline and counsel of one of His people."

Then I go on to say that until we submit to and confide in

someone in the kingdom of God, we are doomed to the tyranny of the self. There is no worse tyrant. Indeed, as we all say, "My worst enemy is myself." Exactly.

So it is far easier to be disciplined by another than to be disciplined by oneself.

And as for counsel, often the worst kind is self-counsel. We are blind and foolish in the assessment of ourselves because of the depth of our egocentricity. It is far safer to be counseled by another person than by ourselves. And if you wish to receive wise, safe and truthful counsel, then you must seek out a Christian who is himself concretely under the authority of God.

Such an arrangement we call a church, "for where two or three are gathered together in my name, there am I in the midst of them" (Matt. 18:20). In this church, composed of two Christians and their Lord, it is now safe to ask for counsel and advice.

All this presupposes that we are willing to have another Christian know us as we really are, allowing this Christian to overhear our confession. Formerly, we confessed our sins to ourselves, hoping that God would somehow overhear these thoughts. Confession to the self is of such little benefit to us and so redundant to the Lord who already knows what we have done, that we should stop calling it confession.

Listen to what Dietrich Bonhoeffer says about confession to the self: "We must ask ourselves whether we have not often been deceiving ourselves with our confession of sin to God, whether we have not rather been confessing our sins to ourselves and also granting ourselves absolution. And is not the reason perhaps for our countless relapses and feebleness of our Christian obedience to be found precisely in the fact that we are living on self-forgiveness and not a real forgiveness?" (*Life Together,* pp. 115-116).

Shepherding is a meeting of the world's smallest church, wherein Christ alone rules and the self is encouraged to be inescapably honest and obedient through the ministry of another Christian. I urge you to turn away from the impossible roads to freedom: self-discipline, self-counsel, self-this, self-that.

Isn't it just like God to surprise us with an easier way?

9

Obedience

A large part of shepherding is simply one Christian lovingly countering another Christian.

That is one of the highest forms of love, to lovingly stand against a person. This is shepherd-love for the sheep.

There is also sheep-love. This love is always an action—the action of doing what the shepherd suggests. Until Sheep A (see Chapter 2) goes on his diet and Sheep B apologizes to that teacher, nothing will happen to change their lives. It all hangs on obedience, not to man, but simply to God.

Now nobody *likes* to be obedient but, having tried everything else and failed, we just may be ready to obey. Fortunately, God does not insist that we enjoy obeying Him. All He asks is that we *do* it.

God's call to obedience has been evaded through the ages and never so much as today. Today in the church, we are too busy to obey. We are easily occupied with refining our doctrines, experiencing the Holy Spirit, spreading the gospel, influencing society, studying the Bible and worshiping the Lord. Do you know that these are all things which the most disobedient among us can easily and happily do? Seldom in all these good practices is a person's will concretely crossed. Sure, I know of some instances where the Word and the Spirit have "cornered" a person, but for every time we are obedient to God through His Word and Spirit, there are many more times where we end up somehow getting our own way again. We always find a way.

It may be that you are one of that vast majority of people in the world today who want only support and approval for what they are doing. They want *no one* to counter them. And as for obedience to a higher authority, who needs it? The higher authorities, including God himself, we are told, are there for no other reason than to assist us in getting what we want. "The reason I need God," said one man to me, "is to help me reach the goals which I have set in life."

If I am describing your viewpoint, I have a request to make.

Please stick with me.

That's all.

You are exactly the kind of person I want as a reader.

10

A Test to See Who Runs Your Life— You or God

Here is a list of ten statements. You find the one which describes your situation in life.

1. *I am under the care of the pastor of my church.*

That sounds like your life is under God's authority, but perhaps only partially because few pastors have the time to really give sustained attention to their parishioners. Also, very few pastors have pastors. The advice you receive from a pastor-less pastor often runs a real danger of being self-oriented.

2. *I don't have any person in particular, but when I have a problem, I do have a few friends with whom I can talk.*

No one denies that the Lord has greatly helped us through our friends. We would surely all be lost without them.

Yet, consider that a variety of friends cannot be expected to keep our heaviest problems confidential. Consider, also, that when we choose to confide in a friend, we are geniuses at selecting just the kind of friend who will almost certainly give hearty support to our ideas. Is not this what we normally expect of our friends?

3. *I am under an elder in my church.*

And who is a shepherd to the elder? Does the elder go to someone regularly for spiritual care? Most elders I know, moreover, contact their sheep when (1) they stop coming to worship and (2) when there is visible trouble. The remainder of the time, you are fairly well on your own.

4. *My wife is my best counselor. God gets through to me through her.*

I'm sure, but remember Adam and Eve. Actually, lovers make poor counselors. They are often the blind leading the blind because they are too close and too invested in each other.

5. *I go to a psychotherapist with my problems.*

Who can afford to do this year after year? But, in addition, of what profit is all this talking which always leaves the patient at the controls of his own life? Where is the psychotherapist who will ask the patient to do something that needs to be done, out of obedience to Jesus Christ? I suspect there are a few such psychotherapists, but I have not yet met them, and I know many.

6. *I simply pray to the Lord and He gives me guidance.*

He may, but the message you receive may sometimes be the hidden thoughts in your own heart. If only you can hear what the Lord is saying, be suspicious. Jesus Christ is never very private. He wants another member of the body around to verify your message.

7. *I study the Scriptures and let them speak to me.*

Most of us practiced egocentrics can get the Bible, when

we are alone with it, to say pretty well what we want it to say. It is true, "the Book reads us," and we do respond, but often selectively and with blindness as to our real needs, which another Christian could point out with no difficulty, except that we do not like other people messing up our neat interpretations.

8. *I am a member of a small sharing group in my church and we advise each other.*

And *you* select the advice which appeals to you most. You've done it again. You've gotten your own way. You run your life.

9. *It's not a question who runs my life—me or God. We do it together.*

Impossible. As impossible as having two people drive a car at the same time. That may last for a few miles, but whose will prevails at the crossroads?

You believe in a god of your own construction, a fantasy-god who never contradicts you.

10. *My work runs my life. My work makes most all the decisions for me.*

Friend, you are still in control of your life. You created a false god and you are hiding behind it in a cowardly fashion. You are in great danger because you are under a delusion that you are a victim of your work when actually you play the almighty as few others do.

The test is finished.

I'm sorry! You flunked the test no matter which of the statements you selected!

You are a clever one! God still has not captured you, you wily egocentric. You've managed to escape Him somehow. You are still on your own—headed straight for possible disaster. When the crises come and the pressure is on you, you will again grab the controls of your life and spin out of control. You are still trying to be in control, as the terrible chaos in your life will testify. Must you always be your highest power?

Come, let us now talk about the specifics of shepherding so that you can make a new statement and pass the test. Here is the new statement:

I am under the spiritual care of another Christian who is himself under my spiritual care. Together we are under God and His Word. We meet regularly and each uses his equal share of time for purposes of confession, advice, guidance and prayer.

Say that, and there will be no question that God is running your life.

11

The Shepherd's Creed

1. From my birth, I have tried to run my own life and I have ruined it.

2. Every possible human resource has been tried to correct my life but all has failed. I have reached the end of my self-life.

3. I have surrendered my will and my life to the Triune God who is the highest power and authority in my life.

4. My submission to God is made concrete by means of five continuing actions.

A. I have placed myself under another person (of my own sex) who has accepted and is practicing this creed with me. We meet on a regular basis. Our time together is equally shared and our roles as shepherd and sheep are exchanged.

B. I practice confession of my sins to God in the hearing of my shepherd whose assurance of confidentiality I trust, and whose assurance of pardon I accept as from God.

C. Having shared my present problems and future plans with my shepherd, I solicit his advice and counsel, believing that the path of obedience to the will of God will be made plain to me through our dialogue.

D. At the beginning of each day, I am taking time, however brief, to absorb the Scriptures and offer prayers to the Lord.

E. I am prepared to share this creed with those who are seriously interested in working this spiritual program.

5. I seek to be surrendered to God in all areas of human life, being nurtured and guided by the local Christian church wherein the Lord has placed me. Within that fellowship, I will be found worshiping, receiving the sacraments, hearing the Word and submitting to ecclesiastical authority.

12

Our Common Disaster

*From my birth, I have tried
to run my own life and I
have ruined it.*

The creed begins with a truthful acknowledgment that
I—and no one else—have wrecked my life. You will see this
only if you acknowledge that you never really were the
innocent battered victim you thought you were, but rather, a
terrible tyrant-giant even as a child. Even today, you want
your way.

Look at yourself.

As a child, you tried to get the world to come to terms with
you. You quickly learned how to handle your parents, either
by a compliance sufficient enough to give the false
impression you were a good child, or by rebelliousness which
walked right over your parents. I myself tried to be a good
child most of the time. My self-centeredness and
omnipotence were always shielded and worked out in
devious ways which still permitted me to get my own way. I
am a brother to a man who once said to me: "I never was in

conflict with my parents. I either lied to them or simply curtained off my life from their view."

Look at what happened in your adolescence. Do you recall the anger with your authorities? Remember your fantasies of yourself as the great and glorious one? Recall how omniscient you were. And competitive. So much of the time, you were impossible to live with. Just ask those who were close to you at that time.

And then, perhaps, you got some education, which richly nourished your egocentricity. Education does that. Education gives us a sense of power to such a degree that frequently, upon the award of an academic degree, the graduate becomes permanently omniscient. He never again learns, he only teaches. Any new facts or even the suggestion that he is wrong he regards as bricks which do not fit into the wall of the kingdom which the self has been so long in building.

Finally, look at the times of trouble throughout your life: the difficulty you have always had with your fantasy life, the numerous addictions which proved you powerless, the conflicts with authorities, the broken promises, conflicts with peers, sexual sins, your vulnerability to fear, your volcanic anger and your wicked tongue, your folly, the wall of loneliness which excluded even God from your world, the people you have hurt and, probably worst of all, the voice of a guilty conscience which will not be silenced.

Enough.

Your life story is my life story. We have all tried, from the day of our births, to run our own lives. Some of us almost killed ourselves. All of us were hurt by our own folly. We ruined the precious, perfect gift of life God gave us.

"All we like sheep have gone astray, we have turned every one to his own way" (Isa. 53:6).

13

The Necessity of Reaching the End of Yourself

*Every possible human resource
has been tried to correct my
life but all has failed. I
have reached the end of
my self-life.*

I am a pastoral counselor.

When a person comes to me for help, I sit down with him and listen closely with my head and my heart.

When the parishioner's life is out on the table, so to speak, I speak to him in this fashion: "Have you exhausted," I ask, "every possibility of help for your problem? Is there another person—a psychiatrist, social worker, psychologist, or another pastor—whom you might like to see before we work together? Are there any books you want to read, organizations you want to join, conferences you wish to attend? Or, is there some new device or technique you wish to yet try?"

When a neurotic parishioner told me she wanted to first try a new tranquilizer, I said: "You go, and when you have swallowed your last tranquilizer, you come back to see me."

Someone else wanted to try massive doses of Vitamin

B-12. "Call me a month after you've finished the treatments," I recall saying to him.

A very earnest person confided in me that he had me as his favorite counselor but he was also seeing his own pastor and a psychiatrist. "I'll wait for them to finish with you," I said, "because I can't stand the competition." Which was not exactly true, so I went on to explain to him that I could not help him until he had given up on everyone else.

A man from AA put it this way: "You won't be ready to receive what we have to offer until you have spent your last buck and shot your last bullet. When you have done that, our door is open to you—and only you can walk through it."

Another time I was watching an old-timer in AA deal with his pigeon (new member). The pigeon said: "I think maybe I've got one or two more drunks in me before I join you boys."

The old-timer drew out his billfold and said: "Here's ten dollars, friend, you go right out now and start boozing. See you later." And with that, the old-timer walked away.

Everyone of us needs to reach the end and face that hard fact. We simply do not get to that point until we have expended all our energy, tried all possible methods, wearied and impoverished ourselves with "help" which is no help at all. Sometimes it takes us a whole lifetime to be emptied, as with the thief on the cross. That man reached the end of himself just in time.

There is no greater tragedy than for a person to find himself on his deathbed, still drunk with plans which cannot work, methods which could never be effective and ideas which never were worthy of consideration. All that should have been abandoned long ago.

14

Let Go—Let God

*I have surrendered my will and
my life to the Triune God who is
the highest power and authority
in my life.*

I recently heard a beautiful story of a mother and her
nine-year-old daughter. One day, the mother asked her
daughter to come to the upstairs bedroom for a talk.

"I want to talk about you and the Lord," she began. "Your
father and I gave you to God when you were baptized. Since
then you have learned about Christ in church and Sunday
school. You know how He stands with you, but now it is time
for a decision on your part. Are you ready to receive Christ
into your life?"

The young girl reflected and quietly said: "I'm ready. I
want Him."

The daughter is now eighteen years old and developing
beautifully as a Christian person. Were she open and candid
about her life, I am sure she would report many doubts,
failings and the problems due to her self-centeredness. Her
surrender to Christ was not complete and, therefore, must be

constantly repeated. But there is no question but that the basic direction of her life was set—and well set—with her mother in that upstairs bedroom, nine years ago. It was the turning point of her life.

Here we have a simple illustration of surrender to God. By God's grace, it may happen when one is very young as in the case of this young girl. It may happen on one's deathbed. I recently ministered to a man who was dying of cancer. He had spent all of his seventy-five years as the highest power and authority in his life. When I found him, he was severely depressed—understandably and deservedly so. I asked him if he was ready to step off the throne and ask God to run his life, now and forever. He was ready. He turned the control of his life over to God.

Surrender is a confession of powerlessness in oneself but of full faith in God.

It is amazing that *anyone* would ever come to a point of surrender in life because so much can go wrong:

• A sense of omnipotence (often created by money and fame) can prevent a person from ever admitting that he is powerless.

• Many come to a point of surrender but then surrender to the wrong power, such as a wife, or child, a business, a sin, or even the occult world.

• There is one group of people who find surrender extraordinarily difficult. They are the traditionally religious. These are people who quote the Scriptures, love the great doctrines of the faith, sing the hymns with feeling, people who like to associate with church people—but never surrender their lives to God. They insist on holding the controls of their lives, and thereby they piously resist God.

• Others surrender to a "God as we understand him" rather than the revealed God who is triune in nature. Human beings love to construct God according to man's image. Such a "god" is worthless. It is not important how we understand God. The important thing is that the Triune God understands us.

I'm tempted to write on and on regarding the intriguing subject of surrender but I must stop. The most important thing is not to talk about it but to do it. If you have come to a point of decision about God, and wish to surrender your will and life to Him, let us now enter into a covenant in the presence of the Lord.

Let us three—the Lord, you and me—agree among ourselves that you are ready to surrender your will and life to the Triune God as the highest power and authority in your life.

The intention of your heart is now set.

But this is not enough. Your profession of faith must be revealed from your own lips to another person.

Perhaps you are prepared now to tell a friend, a spouse, a co-worker, or a pastor of your decision.

Wait. I have an even better suggestion.

Soon, in Chapter 16, you will be shown a simple, effective way to find a shepherd. When you find him, say to your shepherd: "I am ready to take the Third Step of the Shepherd's Creed."

By this disclosure, you will have taken a position, closing down the regime of self-rule and setting your life squarely under the power and authority of Christ in the kingdom of God.

15

Just Do It

*My submission to God is made
concrete by means of five
continuing actions.*

"Turn off the TV set, son, it's time to go to bed."

"Aw, dad, I don't feel like it. It's a good program."

"Turn it off. Time for bed."

"Why, dad? Why can't I see just a little more?"

"Move!" and the father took his son in tow to the bedroom.

Such parenting is rare today. Too bad for our children. Children sorely need parents who will settle only for obedient action.

Children, wanting to control their own wills, will first complain to parents that they "don't feel like it." This is on the level of their emotions.

If the emotions cannot be satisfied, perhaps some satisfaction can be gotten on the level of the understanding. So the child asks, "*Why* can't I?"

All this procrastination and temporizing merely delays the act. Therefore, it is important to go into action first. After that, children will understand why, and still later, they will feel differently.

Now, we adults are the children of God. And God expects the same from us.

First, obedient action. Later, God will give us obedient thoughts and, still later, obedient emotions.

The Lord uses this order—action, understanding, feeling—because it is far easier for us to act (that is, to change our behavior) than to change our thinking and feelings. I recall a woman who had left her husband and then came to me for counsel. She had an airtight argument of "logical" reasons why she should not go back to her husband. I did not try to correct her folly. She was also fiercely hostile with her husband because he was not interested in her. Neither did I deal with these hot emotions. What I did was simply ask her to go back to her husband in spite of her ideas and feelings which, I explained, she had every freedom to keep. All I asked her to do was to go back, for God's sake. I'm happy to say that she went back. The marriage is still in shambles, but it will change because her attitude is changing.

Important as it is to act, I must add that not just *any* action will do. It must be action God wants rather than what we want. Therefore, the suggested action should usually come from outside the addressee. We are frequently much too self-centered and self-deceptive to receive concrete suggestions-unto-action directly from the Lord. Even with a Bible in front of us, we are more prone to listen to ourselves than to it.

It is much less so with a shepherd around.

And if we stay around the Lord by staying around a shepherd, we will avoid a sporadic obedience which is so tedious to the Lord and unproductive in us. We look for a daily surrender to the Lord which issues in continuing obedient action, God guiding us through our shepherd. Cannot God guide us directly? He can and certainly does. But I am recommending here what has become a much neglected way.

Hence, in the Fourth Step, we assert our intention to submit to God concretely by means of five continuing actions—to which we will now turn.

16

Finding a Shepherd

*I have placed myself under another person (of my own sex)
who has accepted and is practicing this creed with me.
We meet on a regular basis. Our time together is equally
shared and our roles as shepherd and sheep are exchanged.*

This is the heart of the shepherding program: "I have
placed myself under another person. . . ."

By such an action, we are greatly assisted in resigning as
Number One. The kingdom of God has no room for two
kings.

Shepherding is a prayerful device whereby we are
concretely subjected to the lordship of Christ through the
agency of another Christian.

"Okay," said a friend of mine, "shepherding is a good idea
based on biblical principles, but answer me one question:
How do I get one of these shepherds?"

"It's really very easy," I said. I went on to tell him that
there are two ground rules he must first understand.

First, the person you ask to become your shepherd must
be of your own sex. This is necessary simply because you
have enough problems without creating new ones. If you

need another reason, consider the fact that your resistance to certain kinds of temptation is ridiculously low. Now isn't that true?

Second ground rule: select a believer in Jesus Christ, no one else. Now don't be endlessly fussy about whether this person is just the right kind of believer for you. Are you not aware by this time how impossible you are to please? If your candidate has confessed Jesus Christ as Savior and Lord, if he is a member of a Christian church, that's enough. Do not insist that he have a stirring testimony, that he speak in tongues, that he be able to pray like a preacher, etc. Even if he had such gifts, he would not be able to use them, busy as he will be with you.

Question:
How do I find a shepherd?

Answer: You hand this book to a likely candidate and say: "Please take this book home and read it. I'm ready to begin working this shepherding program. If you are ready also, let's do it together because it takes two people."

Could anything be more simple? Read the question and answer again.

In this day of crumbling and unstable authorities, we need, as never before, a simple, effective device for the care of our souls. God, through Paul, has answered our needs in saying: "I myself am satisfied about you, my brethren, that you yourselves are full of goodness, filled with all knowledge, and able to instruct one another" (Rom. 15:14 RSV).

With much prayer and a little patience, you can easily locate a like-minded Christian who is ready to begin the program with you.

So the first thing you do is agree to meet.

Where? Not in a restaurant, nor as you take a ride in your car, nor at work, but at your home, face to face.

How? Meet privately, alternating at your home, then the next time at his home. And please, if the TV is on, shut it off. If children or other members of the family are in the room, ask them to leave because the meeting of shepherds is a business meeting, not a social gathering.

When? By appointment, at a time mutually agreeable. My shepherd and I meet for one hour. We divide the time so that each receives thirty minutes. That is to say, he is the shepherd and I the sheep for thirty minutes each. Then we exchange hats so that I am the shepherd and he is the sheep.

How often? At least once a month, but as frequently as daily in times of severe crisis. At the close of each meeting, set the next appointment before you leave. I cannot overstress the need for this. There is no better way to sabotage this good work than to leave each other saying: "I'll phone you later about a future meeting!" It will rarely happen.

My shepherd and I often remark, after our monthly meeting is finished, that we could never go back to the former years when we "flew solo." Those were years of folly, loneliness and well-earned misery. A kind, heavenly Father wants none of that for His children. He desires good things for us—and the only thing keeping us from receiving the fullness of His blessings is our refusal to be under the Word of God which comes through another believer. As Dietrich Bonhoeffer has stated so well, "God has willed that we should seek and find His living Word in the witness of a brother, in the mouth of man. Therefore, the Christian needs another Christian who speaks God's Word to him. He needs him again and again when he becomes uncertain and discouraged, for by himself he cannot help himself without belying the truth. He needs his brother man as a bearer and proclaimer of the divine word of salvation. He needs his brother solely because of Jesus Christ. The Christ in his own heart is weaker than the Christ in the word of his brother; his own heart is uncertain, his brother's is sure'' (*Life Together*, p. 23).

17

Dealing With the Past

*I practice confession of my sins to God in the hearing
of my shepherd whose assurance of confidentiality I trust
and whose assurance of pardon I accept as from God.*

Question:
**I confess my sins directly to God. My sins are nobody
else's business. What's wrong with that?**

Answer: You have done well in confessing your sins privately
to God but it is a sad fact that you are still in the kindergarten
of the school of spiritual maturity. Let me explain five
discernible levels in confessing our sins:

Level 1: *Denial of guilt.* This is a refusal to admit guilt and,
therefore, a refusal to confess. "There is nothing to confess.
I've done no wrong."
Level 2: *Silent confession to oneself.* Here one admits guilt.
The person may not be penitent or sorry for his guilt, but he at
least confesses to himself that what he did was wrong.
Level 3: *Silent confession of sin to God.* My friend, this is

where you are and we thank God for it, but it will be a tragedy if you remain here. You still have not been reunited with the person(s) whom you have sinned against. Neither have you received any good advice from anyone on how to avoid committing the very same sin. Nor have you heard the assurance of God's pardon through the voice of another forgiven sinner.

Level 4: *Verbal confession to God in the presence of a Christian.* Once the confession to God is spoken in the presence of a Christian, the power of sin is broken. My confidant assures me of God's pardon through Jesus Christ. I am loved and accepted, sinner that I am! Now also, I am given good, sound advice which will avoid the twin traps of either excessive atonement for my sin or quickly "forgetting" to right the wrong.

Level 5: *The offer of apology, restitution and peace to the offended person.* All this belongs with any confession to God. Indeed, we may question the sincerity of your silent confession to God on Level 3 if the action of Level 5 is accomplished without the assistance of another Christian on Level 4.

Most Christians get stuck on Level 3 and never use the last two levels. This is like a student who reads 60 per cent of a textbook and then claims to know all there is to know about the course he is taking.

Question:
Why don't Protestants go to confession?

Answer: There are basically two reasons. First, we Protestants prefer to wallow in our sins.

Secondly, we have not had the grace to admit that we made a serious mistake in abandoning the confessional at the time of the Reformation. Our Roman Catholic brethren have since corrected whatever problems there were with the confessional. It is now time for Protestants to return to the discipline of the confessional. Let the confessional first be established among Protestants and later, perhaps, this may serve as part of the bridge which will end our unhappy division.

Question:
I prefer to talk out my problems. Is not that confession?

Answer: No. Not at all. It is probably protection *from* confession.

Confession takes only a few minutes. Problems take forever to explain. This past week a man came to me, wanting to talk about his problem. His problem, he said, was his mother-in-law. He began telling me that she is "a neurotic, old witch who could win a blue ribbon for marriage breaking." After ten minutes, I stopped him because the details of this problem could tie us up for days.

I asked my parishioner to wait a few moments while I wrote something. This is what I wrote: "Dear Mother-in-Law: Once again I find myself taking your moral inventory. I finally am beginning to realize I have a vicious habit of saying only the worst about you. I have pointed to you as the cause of all my problems. Will you forgive me? Please pray for me. I want to live in harmony and peace with you. With my love, John.''

I handed my note to my friend. "Please copy this over and after you have given it to your mother-in-law, call me for your next appointment."

Had I listened passively to this man's problem, it would have taken days. But worse, it would worsen his problems.

Confession is quick and effective. Talking about problems takes forever.

Question:
Is it difficult to confess one's sins to God in the hearing of a shepherd?

Answer: Yes.
Yes.
Yes.

Question:
Exactly what are the benefits of verbal confession?

Answer: The first benfit of this spiritual discipline is that it keeps the confessor honest. The temptation to lie is very strong because of our great difficulty in naming and claiming our sin. The easy way out is to falsify. One may be able to do this silently to himself, but to actually speak the lie and hear it from one's own lips is usually too much for a Christian to bear. He is whipped around by the Holy Spirit to now make a double confession, not only of the "unspeakable" sin but also the lie about it.

Verbal confession, secondly, keeps one humble. Spoken confession destroys pride. It slays us to hear an honest statement of our sins from our own lips. The old man of sin in us dies. This is not mere talk about humility. Nor is it a pious sentiment. It is acted out humility. Such humility cannot be faked, nor can we become proud of such humility.

In the third place, confession into the ear of my shepherd permits him to speak an assurance of God's pardon aimed directly at my confessed sin. My shepherd often says to me something like this: "Earl, God hears you, even as I do. You have confessed the sin of_____. Christ died for your sins and I assure you of His pardon through His blood. Your sin is forgiven. Sin no more."

I have been known to return a few days later to say: "I *still* feel guilty." My patient shepherd again assures me of Christ's pardon. Perhaps he will also add a word of gentle rebuke for trusting my word and doubting Christ's.

In the fourth place, verbal confession opens one to good advice from his shepherd. How can we receive wise counsel unless the shepherd hears the truth?

Finally, true confession ends our loneliness. Sin demands to have a person alone. Confession places us solidly in the forgiven family of God through Jesus Christ.

Question:
What do I confess?

Answer: Begin with little sins. Nail-biting. A heavy right foot when you drive. Tardiness. Overwork. Avoiding worship. Daydreaming. Wasting time on the job. Overeating. Laziness.

Move on to the sins which stick in our throats. Speak the

unspeakable. Take a Bible and look at the Ten Commandments in Exodus 20. Look at a list of the seven deadly sins: pride, envy, anger, sloth, avarice, gluttony and lust.

Finally, always take time to check your resentments. Resentment is a wicked combination of judgment, hatred and revenge. Many of us are literally loaded with resentment. Its targets are infinite: persons, God, self, things, animals, machines, etc. Resentment is spiritual poison. It will burn a hole in us regardless of the target at which it is aimed.

Question:
How can a shepherd forgive my sins?

Answer: A shepherd cannot. Only God can forgive our sins, but we can declare what God has done. No one can pronounce absolution on his own authority, but any believer can and should announce forgiveness when someone confesses his sin to God.

Question:
How often should I make confession?

Answer: Daily, but speaking now about verbal confession, this should be done once a month in the meeting with your shepherd. A good shepherd will ask: "Are there any sins which you wish to confess to the Lord?"

A shepherd, on hearing a confession, may also send his sheep out to confess a wrong to an offended person. With that, however, confession is to stop. It is wrong to continue to confess that sin to a group, to a member of your family, or once again to your shepherd.

Statement:
Frankly, I could never trust another person with my secret life.

Response: We expect the communication between a shepherd and sheep to be quite guarded at first and even superficial. Gradually, however, God gives us trust in and love for the other person. As the relationship continues year after year, you will find there are very few secrets you cannot openly discuss. This is so because your secrets are really no different from your shepherd's secrets. In addition, the exchange of roles at the midpoint of your meeting insures complete safety. My shepherd and I often joke that we each know enough about each other to send us both to jail for life! Since neither of us relishes such a prospect, we keep confidence.

Question:
What if my shepherd and I disagree?

Answer: Your shepherd is not doing his job until he *does* disagree with you. We look for and welcome a clash of wills.

We also look for you to be obedient to the Lord by deferring to your shepherd. You are then a person under discipline, under God's authority. This will not happen until your shepherd counters you in some way and you accept his advice. When this happens, you are not only in the will of God, but also on the road to becoming a free person.

A shepherd should do no more than counter his sheep. It is

not necessary for the shepherd to explain and defend, nor pressure and demand, nor plead and beg. A good shepherd quietly lays his suggested action on the table and quietly waits for his self-willed sheep to come to God's terms.

Question:
What does the Bible say about verbal confession?

Answer: "Therefore, confess your sins to one another, and pray for one another" (James 5:16 RSV).

"He who conceals his transgressions will not prosper, but he who confesses and forsakes them will obtain mercy" (Prov. 28:13 RSV).

"If you forgive the sins of any, they are forgiven; if you retain the sins of any, they are retained" (John 20:23 RSV).

"If two of you agree on earth about anything they ask, it will be done for them by my Father in heaven" (Matt. 18:19 RSV).

Question:
Why must I *hear* that I am forgiven?

Answer: I don't exactly know why, but I do know that until one hears an assurance of God's pardon aimed directly at the sin confessed, one will not really feel forgiven.

Statement:
This all sounds like Catholicism to me. I'm a Protestant and we don't believe in the confessional.

Response: Confession is not something Catholic or

Protestant, it is Christian. Now it so happens that our Catholic brothers and sisters are far ahead of us in practicing confession. Unfortunately, we Protestants abandoned the confessional at the time of the Reformation. It was a terrible mistake. As I look again at the history of the Reformation, I am struck with the unfairness of most of our criticism. Whatever excesses existed at the time have now been largely corrected.

I am hopeful that the idea of shepherding will build a small bridge to Roman Catholic Christians. I realize there are significant differences between the practice of shepherding and auricular (in the ear) confession. Yet both go in the same direction. It is important that we Protestants take the initiative in mending the division we caused by our departure from the Roman Catholic Church.

18

Dealing With the Present and the Future

*Having shared my present problems and future plans
with my shepherd, I solicit his advice and counsel,
believing that the path of obedience to the will of
God will be made plain to me through our dialogue.*

Statement:
I have no problems right now.

Response: When a sheep makes such a statement, it should be
accepted. He may honestly feel quite satisfied with his life.
From where he stands, there are no problems.

You, his shepherd, may not agree. In that case, you should
ask your sheep if he is willing to talk about what you see as a
problem. If the sheep declines the invitation, the shepherd
should not press him.

What you *can* do to help your sheep is set forth your own
problems, clearly and courageously. Your sheep needs a
model to follow, not a wordy sermon.

Question: **What is the goal of shepherding?**

Answer: To find and obey the will of God for my life.

Question:
How does one find the will of God?

Answer: First, you must find God.

The best way to find God is to find a person who knows Him. That person is your shepherd. How can we be sure he knows God? In two ways—he affirms with his words that he is a believer and, secondly he is in concrete submission to God through you as his shepherd. A shepherd represents God to his sheep. That is how we find God.

Having found God, how does one find His will?

Ask your shepherd to *tell* you God's will. He can do this far better than you because he is free from your egocentric bias.

And then *agree with him.*

"If two of you agree on earth about anything they ask, it will be done for them by my Father in heaven" (Matt. 18:19 RSV).

That is how one finds the will of God.

Question:
How can I possibly advise another person—I can't even handle my own life.

Answer: Your pride is plainly visible in that statement. You are again worshiping that image of yourself as a very extraordinary kind of person. With mock humility, you plead that you do not fit into the usual categories. Your special status is based on the false assumption that you must be a person without problems before you can reach out to others.

You appear to be more righteous than others because you demand perfection of yourself before you will help others. You want to be someone special.

Repent.

Ask God to forgive you.

Now, come! Join God's people in helping each other.

Statement:

I like to think my way out of my own problems. A shepherd would only confuse me.

Response: One of the marks of a true egocentric is that he insists on originating all his ideas. Ideas and suggestions from other people are often seen as rude intrusions which confuse the egoist's thinking. By trusting only his own counsel, he cuts himself off from the good counsel of others, and insures his doom.

Statement:

I don't want a shepherd telling me what to do.

Response: Shepherds have no power to command. The only power of the shepherd is a power to suggest. He must lay all his suggestions on the table and then walk away, giving you complete freedom to accept or reject, with no rewards or penalties attached.

Question:

Isn't there a danger of a sheep asking a shepherd to make a difficult decision for him?

Answer: Yes, this is a very real danger. A shepherd can

protect the relationship from this very real trap by suggesting *two* courses of action to his sheep and asking him to choose one.

Not long ago, I said to a high school graduate: "You have a choice, either aim for law school or work in your father's business."

"Which do you think I should do?" he asked, putting me on the spot.

"Let's talk about the advantages and disadvantages of each. That way you'll be able to come to your own decision." I said that because I sensed that this young man was becoming compliant and, hence, irresponsible.

Another way to deal with this problem of overdependency is to openly speak about it. Nothing benefits a sick dialogue so much as Christian candor. A shepherd could say: "I want to check with you whether you are leaning too much on me for your decisions. It is a real danger, you know. What do you think?"

Question:
Isn't there a danger that I may say the wrong thing and cause a nervous breakdown in my sheep?

Answer: Hardly. Normally, a person has a breakdown because his emotional circuits have been overloaded with a high charge of guilt, fear or anger. This painful process usually takes a long period of time. The responsibility for the breakdown cannot be assigned to any particular person who said or did the wrong thing. Breakdowns are not made out of such materials.

Let us think of an extreme case where a sheep is under

great stress. The shepherd sees signs of breakdown in his sheep. It is not necessary to give a list of the signs signaling a breakdown because we all sense immediately when a person is acting strangely and out of pattern. When a shepherd senses his sheep going out of control, he should talk about it and suggest more frequent meetings. This is a time, also, to consult with the pastor of your church.

Question:

If the sheep is breaking down, should not the shepherd get him into a mental hospital as soon as possible?

Answer: Not necessarily.

A shepherd should first do what he can to help his sheep. That may mean frequent meetings at his home, long hours of listening, encouraging the sheep, offering sound advice and conferring with a pastor. In a case where a sheep is suicidal, it may mean that the shepherd would invite the sheep to live in the shepherd's home until the suicidal thinking passes as it does in all but a few cases. If a shepherd stays close to his sheep, and if the relationship is good, it is doubtful that a breakdown will occur.

If you were breaking down, wouldn't you want to be treated that way?

Since things do not always develop according to the neat plans of people who write books, let us suppose the decision is made to enter a psychiatric hospital. In fact, let us suppose that I am the patient. I would hope for three things:

1. I would hope my shepherd would visit me frequently, even every day if possible. I would need him greatly for

advice, prayer and encouragement.

2. I would ask my family to support me in a decision to remain at the hospital briefly, somewhere around two weeks. That is normally enough time to cool down, rest and let the tranquilizers do their work. Soon after discharge, I would ask my physician to take me off of the tranquilizers.

3. Finally, I would ask my family to support me in a decision to decline the use of electroshock treatments. For twenty years I have witnessed both the treatment and the results of the treatment in various mental hospitals. I have no credentials to judge what shock treatments accomplish medically, but I do have a right to an opinion as to whether it is a humane treatment. That I *can* judge. I ask no one else to share my conviction, but in my judgment, shock treatments are clearly inhumane.

Question:
Should I take courses in psychology so I can better help my sheep?

Answer: No, because I strongly discourage you from getting into the role of a psychologist. You are a shepherd, not a psychologist. If you confuse the roles, you will confuse the sheep.

As a shepherd, you offer a spiritual program which lacks no tool to minister to the deepest spiritual needs of a person. Think of Alcoholics Anonymous which is also a spiritual program. Members of AA do not run around asking others for advice on how to handle alcoholics. They *know* alcoholics because they *are* alcoholics. AA people *know* what to do.

You *know* sheep because you *are* a sheep.

We all work a spiritual program.

We do not run off to the professionals to ask for help or for them to tell us what to do. Our Lord did not call us to beg crumbs from the tables of academe. He has called us to sit with Him and eat the Bread of life at His table.

Therefore, by the grace of God, we know what we need to know.

God has taught us how to deal with the central, basic problem in life: self as lord.

There is one problem, and one answer: Jesus Christ as Lord. We have what we really need, thank God. Let us share His food with others, including the psychologists, if they wish to sit at table with us.

Statement:
As a shepherd, I find myself vacillating between being overly cautious and overly bold in my suggestions to my sheep.

Response: I have three suggestions.

1. Never take chances. You *can* do damage. Avoid taking risks.

2. Focus on deeds to do. Don't worry about emotions and intellectual agreement. Recommend deeds done in obedience to Christ. Stick to the possible. Stick to the simple.

I recall a shepherd who, after listening to the details of a stagnant marriage, simply advised his sheep to buy three carnations for his wife. That deed was worth dozens of hours of counsel.

3. With the permission of your sheep, do not hesitate to consult with your pastor.

Statement:

You stress that the shepherd suggest obedient action to the sheep. Give some more examples.

Response: To a man who refused to attend his father's funeral twenty years ago, I suggested that he make the long trip home and place a written apology (which I helped him write) on his father's grave.

To a man who tongue-lashed a car salesman, I suggested he go back and apologize to the salesman.

To Pastor A who deeply resented Pastor B, I suggested that Pastor A mail a book which would be sure to be of interest to Pastor B. This was the first of several actions I suggested in an effort to make peace with Pastor B.

To an alcoholic man who blamed his problem on his wife, I suggested a brief note (which I checked over) offering apology and the hope for reconciliation.

To a confused, floundering man who was greatly discouraged, I simply suggested that he come back tomorrow to again meet with me.

Statement:

I'm a married person and I think that taking advice from a shepherd would drive a wedge between my spouse and myself.

Response: With regard to the relationship of shepherding and marriage, two things should be kept in mind: (1) Married sheep should inform their spouses of the conversation and decisions reached with their shepherds. (2) In any conflict between the authority of a spouse and the authority of a shepherd, the shepherd should defer to the spouse of the sheep. For example, if a wife is counseled by her shepherd to tighten the restrictions on her adolescent son—and the husband disagrees with that decision—the wife should submit to her husband rather than her shepherd. Indeed, even if the husband is *wrong*, his wife should support him in his error of judgment—and vice versa! One should not support a spouse in something clearly immoral, but in errors of judgment, yes, always.

Unless both these suggestions are put into practice, shepherding can become divisive to married people.

Statement:
Sounds good, but I'm still afraid to try it.

Response: Consider, my friend, that you may now know too much to ever again enjoy your apathy.

Remember, too, that at the base of all your fears is a flourishing self-reliance.

Repent of this sin—now—before you lose the opportunity and waste more of your precious life.

Let your reliance be on God alone.

Now let us do His work.

19

Private Devotions

At the beginning of each day, I am taking time, however brief, to absorb the Scriptures and offer prayers to the Lord.

The purpose of private devotions is to correct any wrong attitudes we hold toward God, ourselves, others and the world.

I have a few thoughts on how to have private devotions with delight and profit.

1. READ THE BIBLE until it speaks to a need in you. You will not have to read long.

2. THANK GOD FOR ALL THINGS, especially the crosses, but also the blessings. Name a cross. Name a blessing.

3. ENTER INTO TODAY. Leave the past and future to God. Name the major task of today.

4. EXPECT GOOD THINGS to come from a kind heavenly Father. Let go of fear and pessimism. Name your fear. Picture your deliverance from it.

5. LOOK TO CHRIST as the source of *all* power. Stop

asking Him for a little help with this and that, as if Christ is our assistant. Let Him take charge. We help *Him*. Egocentrics love to ask Christ to help them. He is not our assistant. We are here to do *His* will, *His* work. The power comes entirely from Christ.

6. ASK GOD TO FORGIVE YOUR SINS THROUGH CHRIST. Select and confess a particular sin.

7. FORGIVE YOURSELF and be willing to forgive others. Name one in need of your forgiveness.

8. PRAY FOR YOURSELF, asking God to supply what is needful for your life.

9. FOCUS ON THE NEEDS OF ANOTHER PERSON. Pray for this person and select one need to which you can respond.

10. PRAY FOR OTHERS, using a prayer list.

11. DECLARE YOURSELF A CHRISTIAN. Say the following: "I stand under the grace of God the Father, under the blood of Jesus Christ and under the power of the Holy Spirit."

12. MAKE AN APPOINTMENT with God for devotions tomorrow morning.

20

We Give It Away to Keep It

*I am prepared to share this creed with those who are
seriously interested in working this spiritual program.*

I am hopeful that you and I are in agreement as to the need
for the shepherding program in your life. If it is true that there
is basic agreement between us, you may feel at this point a
desire to share this simple plan of shepherding with others.
Surely, the needs of many people must have come to mind as
you read the preceding chapters.

I beg of you not to do that. This is not a time to run off and
tell everyone about the wonderful idea of shepherding. In
fact, it is not even a time to urge them to read this book.

It is a time for you to work this program.

Begin putting these ideas into practice in your own life. No
one is helped by mere ideas. Naked ideas always cry out to be
clothed in action. Therefore, if you agree with the program I
am suggesting, find yourself a shepherd and test the program
in your own life for at least three months. During that time,
say nothing to others.

Once you are gaining benefit from the shepherding program, then you not only may, but should, speak to others about shepherding. Indeed, your health and growth as a Christian depend upon sharing the program with others. The only way we can keep this gift is to give it away.

Be assured, you will run into plenty of resistance to shepherding. People who have played the king and queen in their lives will not quickly take to the idea of a King (the Lord God) who is concretely represented to them through a shepherd. Be prepared for a person to try many evasive tactics to avoid this "destruction" of his freedom. We must remember that there are many people who would rather die literally, than give up their crazy, mixed-up idea of freedom.

There is no question but that the most fertile ground for shepherding will be God's favorite people, persons who are broken down, in trouble, addicted, physically ill, emotionally ill, lonely, or rejected. A friend of mine calls such "the little people on the bottom of the world." The Lord gathers His people from among those who are "low and despised in the world . . . so that no human being might boast in the presence of God" (1 Cor. 1:28, 29 RSV).

Where there is resistance to the discipline of shepherding, we do not press. Our task is to place the simple idea of shepherding on the table and leave it there. Only God can motivate hearts to receive it. We are beggars telling other beggars where to find the Bread of life.

21

We'll Not Make It Without the Church

I seek to be surrendered to God in all areas of human life,
being nurtured and guided by the local Christian Church
wherein the Lord has placed me. Within that fellowship,
I will be found worshiping, receiving the
sacraments, hearing the Word and submitting
to ecclesiastical authority.

"Shepherding makes sense and is a good program," a friend said to me, "but why must you drag in the idea of the church? Won't shepherding work without the church?"

No, I pointed out, shepherding could never work without the organized church.

Do shepherds feed us the sacrament of Holy Communion as the church does? No.

Can shepherds baptize sheep? Never.

And where in the shepherding program are the Scriptures systematically explained to us? Nowhere.

Where is provision made for regular worship? No provision is made.

Shepherds and their sheep, therefore, would die without the church.

We need the church also to nurture and guide us in applying our Christianity to all areas of life. Our goal as

Christians is not simply to have our souls saved. We want to be told how to make Jesus Christ king in all parts of our lives, in marriage, in daily work, in the nation, in education, in the arts, in our relationships with people, even in our recreation.

There is one more reason why we need the church.

The church gets its authority from God. Because this is so, we who want to be surrendered to God gladly submit to ecclesiastical authority and discipline. We believe this is the path to true freedom.

Indeed, we support *all* legitimate authority.

We teach our children to respect and obey their teachers for no other reason than that the teacher gets his authority from God. In disputes between the teacher and our child, we always support the teacher against the child.

When we get into trouble with the law, we do not recommend that we get a lawyer and go to court. Our aim is to submit to the representatives of the law.

And so with the church. We do not fight ecclesiastical teachings and regulations. We support them, because of the Lord.

22

A Suggested Agenda for Your Meeting

There are seven matters which a good shepherd should raise with his sheep each time they meet.

AGENDA	EXAMPLES
1. Have you done your homework from the last meeting?	"We agreed that I would get a physical check-up and ask my doctor if I was jogging too much. I still have not done it." "Last time I agreed to give up the Tonight Show on TV. I've succeeded."
2. Are there any concerns—joys, sorrows—which you bring to this meeting?	"I'm terribly worried about my money situation." "They gave me a surprise birthday party at work!"
3. Have you said or done anything for which you need God's forgiveness?	"I forgot my mother's birthday." "I had a bad quarrel with my next-door neighbor."

AGENDA	EXAMPLES
4. Do you bear anger and resentment toward any person, group or the Lord?	"I can't stand my minister." "Frankly, God let me down."
5. For what do we need to ask God's guidance and help?	"What should I do about my aged mother?" "My arthritis is killing me. Pray for healing."
6. When can we meet again?	"Let's make it a month from today."
7. Let's pray together.	Father: Thank you for the pardon of our sins through Jesus Christ. I pray for the healing of John's arthritis. Thank you, Lord. We will not be afraid of the future because you possess all power in heaven and on earth. Amen.

23

For Clergymen Only

Dear Pastor:

I am glad to hear that you are happy with the idea of shepherding. You have told me that you are very pleased with a number of things. You like the idea of mutual burden-bearing, even in the case of greatly troubled people. You support a simple, safe way of return to the confession of sins. You appreciate the way the shepherding program is carried on with "only the Lord leading it." Finally, you have told me you are grateful for my solid support of the institutional church, its worship and its mission.

At this moment, you may be thinking of people in your congregation who can use this program. Perhaps names of people come to mind who should be shepherded. They might even be given your copy of the very book you hold in hand.

Stop!

Stop, before you do great harm!

Not a *word* of this to any parishioner.

Please do not say anything about shepherding to your congregation until you yourself are shepherded.

I plead with you to truly lead by your own good example, rather than by words, words, words.

Would you consider, Pastor, that even the pope has a pastor. I am told that the pope goes to his priest every week. There he seeks counsel, shares his problems and asks the Lord for the forgiveness of his sins. Following the pope's good example, every priest in the Roman Catholic Church is required to have his own priest. I am sure some priests rebel against such a rule, but interestingly, most priests I know solidly support the idea and practice of *pastor pastorum*.

Why is it that Protestant clergymen are without pastors? To be sure, the Methodists and Episcopalians have their bishops, the Reformed have their presbyteries or classes and the Baptists have their conferences. To the best of my knowledge, however, our ecclesiastical machinery never even comes close to dealing with the spiritual needs in a pastor's life. We have somehow assumed, I fear, that pastors know so much and are so wise that they can minister to themselves when it comes to spiritual matters. That, as you know, is nonsense! We are not the gods we often pretend to be. Pastors are sheep first of all, and sheep need shepherds.

If you, as a man under God, will come under God's authority vested in another pastor, then you will be in a position to recommend shepherding to your people.

I am writing these words in late November, the thanksgiving season. I have new reason now for joy and thanksgiving as I think of the rich, spiritual harvest which awaits you and your people. We all have often prayed for a deeper spiritual life and a new commitment to our Lord. Shepherding is one of a number of ways through which the Lord will surely answer these prayers.

Cordially in Christ,

Earl Jabay

24

How to Begin

If you are convinced that every Christian needs a Christian, then it is time to begin.

Let us first go to the Good Shepherd. Ask our Lord to direct your mind to someone who might become your shepherd and you, his sheep.

He should be a Christian.

He should be one of your own sex.

These are the only restrictions to keep in mind.

Guard against that old tendency in you to be finicky, fussy and so difficult to satisfy. You have suffered sufficiently for these sins, why ask for more punishment? Really, most any Christian will do.

And please, do not deliver a lecture to your candidate on "The Theory and Practice of Shepherding." If you lecture, you will lose him.

Just hand him this book.

Ask him to read it, and if he is interested in becoming a shepherd, you would like to work with him.

And one more thing.

Agree on when you may expect his decision.

A week?

Two weeks? That should be time enough to read a book of this length.

Then you contact him for his decision, and, hopefully, an appointment to meet together to begin the most profitable journey of your life.

NOTES

NOTES

NOTES

NOTES

NOTES

NOTES

NOTES

NOTES

NOTES

For free information on how to receive
the international magazine

LOGOS JOURNAL

also Book Catalog

Write: Information - LOGOS JOURNAL CATALOG
Box 191
Plainfield, NJ 07061